LANCASHIRE
LIMERICKS

by
John Sephton

LANDY
Publishing

Landy Publishing
"Acorns"
3 Staining Rise
Staining
Blackpool FY3 0BU
Tel/Fax: 01253 886103

Landy Publishing have also published:-

Valley Verses : Dialect poems by Margaret Helliwell

Lancashire Laugh Lines : Humorous verses by Kay Davenport

In Lancashire Language : Dialect verses edited by Bob Dobson

In Fine Fettle : Dialect verse by Michael May & Peter Thornley

Woven in Lancashire : Dialect poems edited by Bob Dobson

A full list of publications will be sent on request.

ISBN 1 872895 22 0

Designed and produced by Coveropen Ltd.
Tel: (0524) 534578

Printed and bound in Great Britain.

INDEX/GAZETTEER

INDEX/GAZETTEER

ACCRINGTON

A 'omin'-pigeon fancier fro' Accrington
'Ad a cropped white-ringt brid and a black-ringt un;
Cropped brid 'ad to walk,
So 'e learned it to talk,
An' ask folk best road back to Accrington.

ARRAD FOOT

A young sweep from o'er Arrad Foot
Used to walk about covered i' soot;
His typist-friend, Poppy,
Got a good carbon-copy
As covered the lass head-to-foot.

ASHTON-IN-MAKERFIELD

A farmer from Ashton-in-Makerfield
Sampled t' crop from his big new tobakkerfield;
Some, in his opinion,
Were Turkish, some Virginian,
But most were plain Ashton-i'-Makkerfield.

ATHERTON

To a lass gath'rin' rosebuds i' Atherton
A toff gi' a bought 'un fer each gathert 'un;
Sayin' "Please: just one kiss
For these rosebuds, please Miss,"
She said, "Oppit, 'oo wants ter be slavert on?"

BACUP

A flighty young madam fro' Bacup,
When her Dad said she used too much macup,
Ran away in a huff,
Began to live ruff,
And said, "Time our old chap had a shacup."

BAILRIGG

A brainy old chap fro' Bailrigg
Were being fit wi' a National Health wigg;
He said, "It's too small,"
They said, "Nay, not at all,
It's thi' head's seven sizes too bigg."

BANKS

A motorist, living i' Banks,
Said, "Ah've getten a horn as ne'er honks;
Each time Ah press button
Damn thing's dead as mutton:
Still, it's better nor if th' 'ingine conks."

BARROW-IN-FURNESS

Said an artiste from Barrow-in-Furness,
"Stage leets is that breet they can burn us;
Tha'll see, in me sand-dance,
And t'wife's Eastern fan-dance
How brown they're beginning to turn us."

BICKERSTAFFE

A brazent lass living near Bickerstaffe
Said at Jones's, "Any stuff t'match these knickers, Taff?"
Taffy shouts for his Mrs
An says, "Show this lass thrs
Best drapers for knicker-stuff round Bickerstaffe."

BILLINGE

A plump amateur actress fro' Billinge
Thought her part in the pantomime thrilling;
They'd said, "Will you play Crusoe
In tights? Please, please do so,
The part takes a great deal of filling."

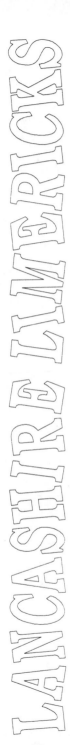

BLACKBURN

Coming home wet, a feller fro' Blackburn
Smelt his warming-up suppertime snack burn;
When he yelled for his daughter
She dowsed him wi' waughter,
She'd thought he'd let th' 'em of his mac burn.

BLACKPOOL

A dreamy young lady fro' Blackpool
Read that novel by H. de Vere Stacpoole;
It drove her near frantic,
A place so romantic
As t'Blue Lagoon weren't nearer Blackpool.

BOGGART HOLE CLOUGH

A feller fro' Boggart Hole Clough
Decided to start tekkin' snough;
It's his sneezes, they reckon,
Caused all t' boggarts to weckon,
And come swarmin' like snigs out o't' Clough.

BOLTON-LE-SANDS

A big chap fro' Bolton-le-Sands
Plays trombone, but's to watch how he stands;
A bit on one side,
He clouts next chap wi't' slide,
T'other road an' he flattens t' music-stands.

BOOTLE

A patient young lady fro' Bootle
Thought th'Intended's behaviour were brootle;
She said, "Wouldn't it be t' thing
To give me a ring?"
He said, "Reet, lass, Ah'll gi' thee a tootle."

BORWICK

Some superior folks living in Borwick
Were boasting the place were historwick,
But the Borwick Hall Ghost
Said, "There's no need to bhost,
It won't never get thee nowheer i' Borwick."

BROWN EDGE

There was an old chap fro' Brown Edge
Who were found in a barn, on a ledge;
They said, "What's this about?"
He said, "T'wife's chucked me out,
Ah hope it's not thin end o't'wedge."

BURNLEY

A Scouser, when visiting Burnley,
Had to say to a taxi-man, sturnlee,
"I'm astonished you dur
Ask for such a big fur;
It's not Liverpule, this, onlee Burnlee."

BURY

There was a young farmer, near Bury,
Who used to buy fish, chips and curry
To eat up on t' fell;
He said, "Aye, there's a smell,
But no worse nor a tankload o' slurry."

CABUS

A colour-blind feller fro' Cabus
Could ne'er tell a green from a grabus;
Trying to bus it to Grange
He made a wrong change
And fetched up instead back i' Cabus.

CARK

There was an old feller fro' Cark,
Said his dog could see burglars i' t' dark;
When they said, "Oh, give over,"
He said, "And, moreover,
Ah've getten a cat as can bark."

CATON

An unlucky young lass out o' Caton
Had to slim when she put too much waton;
She got herself thin,
But said, "Hee, you can't win,"
When she fell down a gratin' i' Caton.

CHARNOCK RICHARD

An old chap fro' near Charnock Richard
Said, "Sithee, me hens has bin butchert!
Except for them cocks;
It must be yon focks
What's bin prowlin' around Charnock Rutchert."

CHAT MOSS

A naggin' owd wife fro' Chat Moss
Found th'owd chap had run off wi' his noss;
She'd nobbut 'a' laughed
To hear owt so daughed,
But th' owd divil had tekken her poss.

CHORLEY

There's a sweet bonny lass comes fro' Chorley
Who all t' lads fell i' love with, reet sorely;
One said, "Oh, the bliss,
If tha'd give me one kiss,"
She said, "Hop it, tha makes me feel porely."

CHORLTON-CUM-HARDY

A young chap fro' Chorlton-cum-Hardy
Were that soft, some folks called him a mardy;
But he grew up that tough
He'd go out in a hough,
And separate Chorlton from Hardy.

CHURCH

A bride wi' no groom at Church church
Sniffed, "Reckon Ah've bin left i't' lurch lurch;
'E's nobbut a lad lad,
Not really bad bad,
But 'e wants knockin' off 'is purch purch!"

CLAYTON-LE-MOORS

A feller fro' Clayton-le-Moors
Got confused, and went knocking on doors;
They said, "Henry, Good Heavens!
Th'art at sixes and sevens!"
He said, "Nay, nobbut threeses and foors."

CLAYTON-LE-WOODS

A bridegroom fro' Clayton-le-Woods
Promised t' bride he'd share all wordly goods,
Except for his car,
His hi-fi, his guitar,
His gowd watch and his cufflinks and stoods.

CLEVELEYS

A fussy owd feller fro' Cleveleys
Said to t' wife, "There's a spot on thi sleeve, Liz:"
She said, "Look, it's a spider,
Knock it off an' don't mider,
Th'art fussiest owd fogey i' Cleveleys."

CLITHEROE

A hesitant youth living i' Clitheroe
Could ne'er decide nowt, a reet ditherer;
Till his dad said, "Hey, thee;
Just decide **summat**, see,
If only to hop it out o' Clitherer."

COLNE

A serious young feller fro' Colne
Used to go on long bike-rides alolne;
Till a lass who said, "Sithee,
I'd like to come withee,"
Made him grin like a dog wi' a bolne.

DARWEN

An owd chap as farmed above Darwen
Would alwa's leave furthest field barren;
When folks asked him, Why,
He would say, wi' a sy,
"Ah've getten plenty to do nearer Darren."

DELPH

A sensible lass out o' Delph,
Who'd been happy to be left on the shelph,
Reckoned it just a bit funny
When she come into munny,
How men loved, not her brass, but herselph.

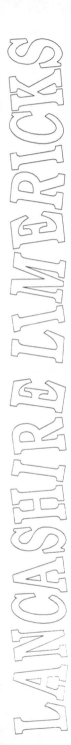

ECCLES

There's a merry lass living i' Eccles
Whose arms and neck's covered i' freccles;
When t'lads bets she won't show
Just how far down they go,
She says, "Nay? Just thee show me ten sheccles."

ELLEL

A lad, doing his homework at Ellel,
Asked his dad, "Does ta know 'ow to spell 'ell?"
"Wi' a haitch, thee don't drop it,"
Said dad, "or tha'll cop it,
An' I 'opes tha'll ne'er 'ear, see nor smell 'ell."

EUXTON

A worthy owd feller from Euxton
Got a job at a church as a seuxton;
Digging grave number two,
He said, "This'll not dwo,
Ah feels fit ter be buried i't' neuxton."

FAZACKERLEY

An eager young chap fro' Fazakerley
Clocks off at four-thirty exakerley;
He opens his wages,
Then counts 'em for ages,
And says, "New notes is so nice an' crakerley."

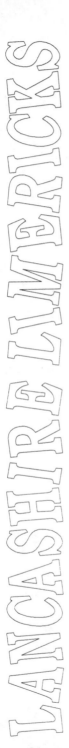

FLEETWOOD

He said, this young feller fro' Fleetwood,
"Nowt'd shift me off oppen trams," but sleet would;
He'd pull the tram-trolley
Off the wire wi' 'is brolley,
An' dive for a shelter afore t' street flood.

GATEACRE

A rough sort o' family i' Gateacre
Had a mongrel folks thought were a tatty cur;
But when t' lad fell i' t' Mersey
It cetched 'im bi t' jersey
An' fetched 'im 'ome drippin' ter Gateacre.

GLASSON

A cheeky young lass out o' Glasson
Told a lad, "This zip's stuck, it won't fasson;
Will you look if it's bustin'?
Me eye's got some dust in;"
"Which one?" he said, "real un or t' glasson?"

GRANGE

An operatic lady fro' Grange
Has a voice as is powerful and strange;
There's a note she can render
Rattles fire-irons on t'fender
And clears flues i' th' owd kitchen range.

HAIGH

There was a young feller fro' Haigh
Whose ideas of being honest were vaigh;
He was doing folks down
Just all over the town,
They avoided him soon like the plaigh.

PUT SOME SKIN ON,
AFORE THA CATCHES
THI DEETH O' COWD,
THA BONY OWD DIVIL—
AN' DON'T SCREET!

HEAPEY

A lad found cheap lodgings near Heapey
In a haunted house, lonely and creapy;
He towd t'ghost one neet
When it give a gret screet,
"Don't moither, owd lad, Ah'm too sleapey."

HEATON PARK

A young chap fro' near Heaton Park
Met a saucer-eed dog in the dark;
It were lickin' some yoghurt
Just like real, not a boghurt,
But it mizzled and left nowt but a spark.

HESKETH

A dressy young feller fro' Hesketh,
When asked why he wore a plaid weskit,
Said, "Ah likes the thing, see?"
They said, "Does it like thee?"
He replied, "It's ne'er said, but Ah'll esk it."

HEYSHAM

A notice at park gate at Heysham
Says, "Them as walks dogs 'ere mun leash 'em,
An' 'owd the leash tight
To mek sure they don't bight.
Signed, His Worship the Lord Mayor of Heysham."

HINDLEY

Not mony folks could tek kindly
To an owd chap fro' t' place 'e co'ed Hindley;
He'd say, "Is that thi face?
Well, it looks a disgrace
Tha looks no better frontly nor behindly."

HOLKER

A thin-blooded house-guest at Holker
Tried to warm 'is cowd feet in the colker
But they turned th' 'eat up high
And 'e shot in the skigh
As though from a discharged bazooker.

HOLME

A Burnley chap, livin' at Holme,
Could part his hair once, wi' a colme;
But now, 'e's reet galled
'is 'ead's gone that balled
It favvers a pink marble dolme.

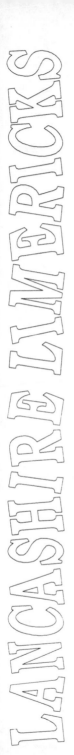

HUTTON

There was an owd feller fro' Hutton,
Who liked beef a lot better nor mutton;
When 'is wife said, "It's dearer,"
He'd frame not to 'earer
Bi studyin' 'is top weskit button.

KENYON

An 'ard-up owd feller from Kenyon
Towd t' daughter 'e lived wi', "There's menyon
Owd feller today
Pays tuppence fer a tay,
It's gettin' bad findin' a penyon."

KNOTT END

A madcap young driver o' Knott End
Kecked o'er 'is fast car on a bend;
He were chucked reet on t'ferry,
And said, "Sorry fer the herry,
Ah'll pay for mi trip t'other end."

LANGHO

There was a young feller fro' Langho
Who were expert at dancin' the tangho;
To say that 'is waltz
Were as good, would be faltz,
But 'e's o'reet at doin' a fandangho.

31

LATHOM

An owd chap as walked 'ere fro' Lathom
Stuck 'is feet in a bucket to bathom;
When 'is toes o' tornt blue,
He said, "What a rum do."
An' offed back wi' 'is bucket to Lathom.

HEALEY

There was an owd feller fro' Healey (yelly)
Said, "There's such a bad pain i' mi' bealey;
'Appen summat Ah've getten
Through summat Ah've etten,
Ah'm shakin' all o'er like a jealey."

LEIGH

A chap wetchin' t' rugby at Leigh
Said to t' chap in front, "Shift; Ah cawnt seigh."
"Ah'm t' linesman, tha crackpot,"
Says t' chap, "tha teks jackpot
Fer 'avin' less brains ner a fleigh."

LITTLE LEVER

A wife as lived o'er Little Lever
Chased 'er nervous owd chap wi' a cleaver;
When t' blade bust 'is braces
Some folks wi' red faces
Held 'er back while 'e threatened 'e might leave 'er.

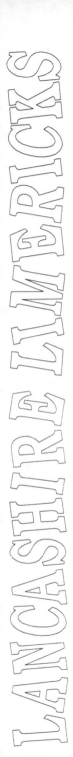

LYDIATE

There's a young lad at schoo' theer i' Lydiate,
He's that little, 'e's no more ner a mydiate;
But 'e meks up i' n'ise
What 'e's lackin' i' size,
'Cause 'e's ne'er still, 'e's such a young fydiate.

LYTHAM

An amateur band went to Lytham,
And took all their instruments wytham;
An ancient kazoo,
A mouth-organ or too,
And a side-drum to tap out the rytham.

MELLOR

There was an owd chap lived i' Mellor
Who took widder next door down i't' cellor;
Folks yelled down, "What ta doin'?"
He said, "Billin' an' cooin',
An' if tha sees t'wife, never tellor."

KISS ME

MERE BROW

There was a young chap fro' Mere Brow,
Who got 'issel' tossed bi a cow;
It 'ooked 'im bi t' britches
An' jumped o'er ditches
Till 'e got cetched on a mistletoe bough.

MESNES

A Wigan lad, livin' at Mesnes,
Met a boggart comin', rattlin' it' chesnes;
Lad said, "Hey, 'owd thi row,"
Boggart said, "Thee tell me 'ow,
When Ah'm shiverin'-cowd, 'as t' no bresnes?"

MORECAMBE

Said a Lancashire chap, visitin' Morecambe,
"Folks is bad 'ere, Owd Nick should pitchforecambe
Down to t' Regions Beneath,
Wheer there's gnashin' of teath,
O' these Yorkshire folk, livin' i'Morecambe."

MUCH HOOLE

An elderly chap fro' Much Hoole
Nearly drowned when 'e fell in a poole;
They said, "Ha'n't ta sin t'warnin'?"
He said, "Aye, ev'ry marnin',
But Ah cawn't read, Ah ne'er went to schoole."

MUMPS

An Oldham chap, livin' i' Mumps,
Said, "Eh, dear; A'm reet down i' t' dumps;
Wife's sister's got builder in,
Oo's stoppin' wi' t' chuilder in
Our 'ouse an' it's tumblin' i' lumps."

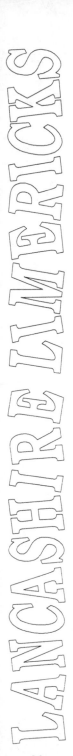

NELSON

Late at neet once, a young chap fro' Nelson
Met a ghost, wailin' "Save me from 'ell, son!"
Lad said, "'eigh, not so loud:
I' yon mucky owd shroud
They'll ne'er 'ave thee, put summat else on."

NETHER KELLET

An 'owd lass from o'er Nether Kellet
Knew a tale but she never would tellet;
When they said, "Write it down,"
She replied, wi' a frown,
"I would if I could, I can't spellet."

NEWTON-LE-WILLOWS

A feller fro' Newton-le-Willows
Went a sail and were reet bounced i' t' billows;
It med 'im that sick
He come home hardly wick,
And had to be propped up wi' pillows.

NORTH MEOLS

A merry young lass fro' North Meols
Used to like wearin' very high heols;
When she fell down a sough
Full o' rubbish an' stough,
They found 'er by following her squeols.

OLDHAM

A fierce army-sergeant from Oldham
Yelled at rookies that 'ard 'e reet cowed 'em;
When they wrote a complaint
He said, "Fancy: 'Ow quaint:'
An' towd 'em Queen's Regs ne'er allowed 'em.

ORMSKIRK

A lodging-house keeper in Ormskirk
Said, "Eh dear; 'ow these Russians fro' Tomsk irk
A woman like me,
Expectin' for t' tea
Fresh caviare-on-toast 'ere in Ormskirk."

ORRELL

A pleasant young lady from Orrell,
Whose beads were a nice plastic correll,
Now gets 'ome wi' t' milk,
Dressed i' diamonds an' silk;
Folks is startin' to wonder if she's morrell.

OSWALDTWISTLE

There were a young feller fro' Ozzletwistle
As played tunes on 'is grondod's three-nozzlt whistle;
One nozzle played low notes
An' one not-so-low notes,
An' one played as 'ee as a throstle's whistle.

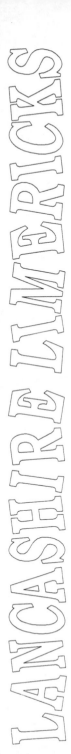

PADIHAM

Two lively young lads out o' Padiham
Went off wi' some golfers to caddy 'em,
When one drove off t' course
Ball were swallered bi a hourse,
An' t' lads drove off i' t' cart back to Padiham.

POULTON-LE-FYLDE

An owd chap fro' Poulton-le-Fylde
When talkin' to folks often smylde,
And when asked what it meant
Said he lived in a teant,
And were 'appy the weather were mylde.

PRESTON

There was a young feller fro' Preston,
Lost a navy-blue trilby, 'is beston;
But it weren't lost, because
He knew just wheer it wause;
On a train on the London North Weston.

QUERNMORE

A knight wi' a castle i' Quernmore
Said, "Ah wish this 'ere castle were warmer;
If Ah shifted ter Bolton
Ah'd bi warmer wi nowt on
Thah 'ere, i' this thick suit of armour."

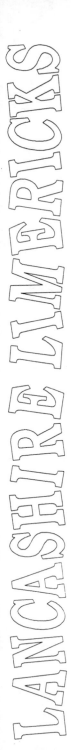

ROCHDALE

A man-mad   young madam fro' Rochdale
Ran away, but they went off an' catched 'er;
They said, "Never again
Will tha chase after main,
Or we'll only chase thee, back ter Ratchder."

ROSSALL

There was a young feller fro' Rossall
Whose love for all birds was colossall;
He retrieved in one day
Two lame ducks and a jay,
A bad girl and a gull and a throssall.

RUFFORD

A mis'rable owd woman fro' Rufford
Kept grumblin', "Think on 'ow Ah've sufford;"
When they'd suffered enough grumblin'
They o' started tumblin'
O'er each other ter get out o' Rufford.

ST. ANNES

Two sisters who lived in St. Annes
Used to send coupons for free pots and pannes;
Pru wouldn't get caught
When she found she was shaught,
Instead of her own she St. Annes.

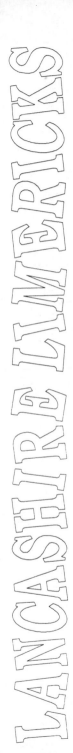

ST. HELENS

They said to a stranger i' St. Helens,
"Nah, what's o' these sniffin's an' smellin's?
If tha don't like the place,
Well, don't poo such a face,
Just 'op it off out o' St. Helens."

ST. MICHAEL'S ON WYRE

A chap fro' St. Michaels on Wyre
Turned 'is thermostat yre and yre,
Till one verra cowd neet
His poor wife got a freet
When 'e fled wi 'is britches afyre.

SCARISBRICK

A stubborn young builder fro' Scarisbrick
Hated stone, but did nowt but praise brick;
But 'e praised it no more
When 'is 'ouses fell ore,
He give up, and settled i' Scarisbrick.

SEFTON

A young learner-driver fro' Sefton
Ne'er knew 'er reet 'and from 'er lefton,
And when t' chap said, "Turn reet:"
Smashed a two-ton iron seat,
And 'er little round chin kissed 'is clefton.

47

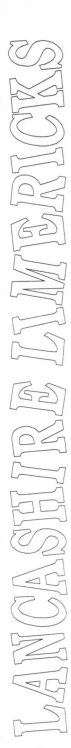

SLYNE

A crooked young feller fro' Slyne
Ne'er knew t' difference between myne an' thyne,
Thinkin' what wasn't, were his'n,
Till they put 'im i' pris'n,
Bout the option, they said, of a fyne.

SOUTHPORT

A man in a hotel in Southport
Said, "It makes me feel down in the mouth, port;
I get merry on perry,
And on sherry I get verry,
Fit to dance i' France, if not i' Southport."

STANDISH

There was a young feller fro' Standish,
Who carried on summat outlandish;
He would tee a balloon
To each on 'is shoon,
And dribble 'em all o'er Standish.

STODDAY

She towd t'lads, this young madam fro' Stodday,
She'd a serpent tattooed round 'er bodday;
When one called 'er a liar,
She said, "Sithee: a bit hiar:
Here's a tail on mi leg, tha gret nodday."

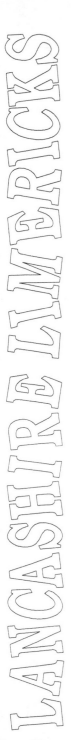

THURNHAM

Some men plantin' signposts at Thurnham
Just didn't know which road to turnham;
They asked mony a chap,
But not one 'ad a map,
So they said, "Chop 'em up an' we'll burnham."

TONGE

A noisy young lad out o' Tonge
Used to whistle while traipsin' along;
When folks didn't like it,
He said, "Reet then, Ah'll bike it,"
Stopped whistlin', an' bust into songe.

TORRISHOLME

Late one neet, a young feller fro' Torrisholme
Escorted his young lady Doris holme;
When a big chap come out
And give him a clout,
She said, "Next time, we'd best beat our Horace holme."

TREALES

An unlucky owd racegoer fro' Treales
Bet on 'orses as o' run like sneales;
Till at 'Aydock, 'e won,
An' said, "That were good fon,
Ah feels just like a dog wi' two teales."

TROUGH OF BOWLAND

A chap as lived up Trough o' Bowland
Asked a Dutchman, "Ain't this better nor Holland?"
Chap said, "What, Bout canals?
Bout windmills? Bout mi pals?
An' it's reet nice an' flat theer in 'Olland."

TRUB SMITHY

When two oil-chaps, browt up i' Trub Smithy,
Cum back theer fer good, one says, "Sithy:
Wi' new motorways all o'er it
There's nothin' else fo'er it;
If tha'll go back to Bahrain, Ah'll cum withy."

WHITTLE-LE-WOODS

A daft chap fro' Whittle-le-Woods
Jumped on t' train and said, "Nay! it's a Goods!"
An' t' cows, stood i' t' van,
Said, "Nay! it's a Man!"
And stood starin' theer, chewin' their coods."

WIDNES

Some burglars who'd come o'er fro' Widnes
Said, "We're lucky this dark neet 'as idnes;"
But some bobbies o'er t' wall
Said, "It 'id us an' all;
Just come i' this van back to Widnes."

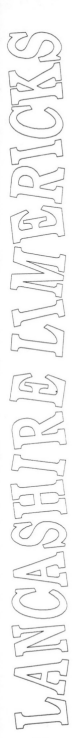

WIGAN

A frustrated owd chap, stuck i' Wigan,
Were besotted wi' dreams o' New Biggin;
To work off 'is besotment
He'd go on th' allotment
An' start diggin' an' diggin' an' diggin'.

WINWICK

A mis'rable pet-owner fro' Winwick
Had to take 'is sad monkey to t' clinwick;
They said, "Trouble wi' this groaner
Is nowt but its oaner,
A monkey were alwa's a mimwick."

WISWELL

There was an owd feller fro' Wiswell
Who fell o'er a big prickly thiswell;
He said, "By Gum, that 'urt,
An' Ah've torn mi good shurt,
An' Ah'm weet, sin' it cum on ter driswell.

WREA GREEN

A popular lass o' Wrea Green
Always tastefully dressed in grey-green;
Her name was Irene,
To some she was Reenie,
And some called her just a vague Reen.

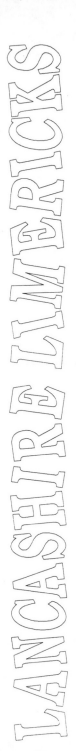

YEALAND

A love-struck young feller fro' Yealand
Towd t' girl's dad 'e'd struggle through ealand
High water
Ter marry 'is dater;
Her dad said, "Yer o' daft, i' Yealand."

YEWDALE

There once were a farmer i' Yewdale
Used ter round up 'is sheep wi' a poodle;
They got mixed up at shearin'
Wi' t' poodle appearin'
O' sheeplike, an' t' sheep like a poodle.